"This is the best material I've see~~n~~
ing what's in the Bible and how it

—Justin Taylor,
Crossway and The Gospel Coalition

"*Clarifying the Bible* is an AMAZING resource! I've seen
personally, from a small group setting to one-on-one, how this
resource can open up your understanding of God's Word in a
way that drives you to want more of Jesus.
My wife and I love it!"

—Tedashii,
Hip Hop Artist, Reach Records

"We are all aware of the growing phenomenon of biblical
illiteracy. Mitch Maher has set out to address this problem. His
overview, *Clarifying the Bible*, indeed clarifies the whole Bible. He
is a clear and likable communicator, and he knows his stuff. May
the Lord use Mitch and this project to turn the tide of
biblical illiteracy!"

—Jim Hamilton,
Professor of Biblical Theology, Southern Seminary

"For college students, I haven't found a more clear and concise
resource that gives such a solid framework through which to
understand the story line and structure of God's Word than
Clarifying the Bible. I've had Mitch come teach at our summer
training projects, shown his video in countless
discipleship groups, taught these principles and lessons several
times, and I still want more!"

—Taylor Tollison,
Area Director, Campus Outreach, University of Tennessee

"I grew up in church, son of a pastor. I have worked in churches for years and paid quality money for a fantastic seminary education. And yet, no resource has so concisely framed the narrative of Scripture as Mitch's work in *Clarifying the Bible*. I watch it regularly. I teach it often. I have given this to many leaders and friends. It should be in the hands of every follower of Jesus that they might know, teach, and embody the Gospel more and more."

—Will Rambo,
Senior Pastor, The Orchard, Tupelo, MS

"Mitch brings incredible clarity to the entire Bible in a way that gives both new believers and seminary graduates a greater ability to comprehend and appreciate God's Word. I gained more understanding in two hours of *Clarifying the Bible* with Mitch than in my previous 10 years studying the Word on my own. This is a treasure for those who are hungry to know their Bibles."

—Kennon Vaughan,
Founder, Downline Ministries, Memphis, TN

"One of the greatest needs of our day is a working knowledge of the biblical story. Mitch Maher not only knows it, but he has put it down in understandable terms and flow. Anyone who reads/watches *Clarifying the Bible* will come away with a lifelong framework to understand the Bible."

—Tom Nelson,
Senior Pastor, Denton Bible Church, Denton, TX

"You don't need a seminary education to have strong biblical muscles. One of the best places to start is with a good overview that familiarizes you with the Scriptures as a whole.
Mitch Maher can get you there quickly and effectively.
His media experience, *Clarifying the Bible*, will turn God's Word into a good friend that you'll look forward to spending time with every day… for the rest of your life."

–Tim Kimmel,
Author of *Grace Based Parenting*

"*Clarifying the Bible* is a marvelous resource, which provides the big picture context of the whole story of the Bible and understanding for how the various parts fit together. Mitch Maher hits the mark identifying a common reason why many 'would be' students of the Bible quickly get discouraged and abandon their goals AND provides a non-intimidating solution that not only gets them started, but also continues to help them the whole way through. Whether you are a novice or a seasoned student of the Bible, *Clarifying the Bible* is a tool you will refer back to often. In less than two hours, Mitch walks you through the entire Bible showing you how it flows and fits together. He provides a simple yet thorough overview without watering it down, whetting your appetite for further study of the Bible. I wish I'd had this as a resource when I was entering seminary! We now provide a copy for every woman entering Denton Bible Church's Women's Discipleship Training Program (where we seek to equip an average of 20-24 faithful women to serve the Lord in whatever avenues He opens up to them for the rest of their lives). The most common response I hear from our students is 'Aha!' as the framework Mitch presents helps them fit the pieces of the Bible together into one story."

–Jean Klughart,
Director, Women's Discipleship Training Program,
Denton Bible Church, Denton, TX

"*Clarifying the Bible* has turned the lights on for countless aspiring disciple makers participating in the Downline Institute. The brilliance of this tool is that it is at the same time simple and robust, theologically deep yet reteachable, and its progression and flow build the confidence of the learner. It is no wonder this tool is being taught by pastoral and lay leaders all over the world. I've rarely made it six months with a young protege without equipping them with *Clarifying the Bible*."

–Danny Hinton,
Executive Director, Downline Ministries, Little Rock, AR

"There is no question that biblical ignorance leads to a multitude of sins. Behind biblical ignorance is often an intimidation of the Bible itself. *Clarifying the Bible* goes to war with that intimidation and equips and frees men and women to engage the Scriptures with a passion and freedom. It's a powerful presentation and inspires all who hear it to make biblical study a lifelong passion. I've personally seen people move from biblical apathy to passionate students of God's word after engaging Mitch and *Clarifying the Bible*. Exciting stuff!"

–John Bryson,
Lead Pastor, Fellowship Memphis Church, Memphis, TN
Consultant, Fellowship Associates, Little Rock, AR

"I highly recommend Mitch Maher's *Clarifying the Bible*. It is a unique resource that succinctly brings together valuable information about the Bible's message and theology. I have used the material with great profit in our home and in many classes at our church. Church leaders will appreciate that it is well-researched and warmly presented for the people of God."

–Dr. Paul S. Lamey,
Pastor, Grace Community Church, Huntsville, AL

"The current generation of college students is one marked by misconceptions of true Christianity, biblical illiteracy, and the inability to quiet the mind and sit still. *Clarifying the Bible* is an effective resource in helping new Christians coming out of this context to understand the Great Story from beginning to end. Mitch presents it in a personally engaging and concise way, which is appealing to this easily distracted generation.
I will enthusiastically use it for years to come!"

—Michael Cody,
Campus Outreach Campus Director,
University of North Alabama

"Every Christian knows that reading the Bible is fundamental for spiritual growth. However, many of them find the Bible intimidating and difficult to understand. As promised, Mitch helped clarify the Bible and gave those in attendance a helpful and clear framework to better understand the story of the Scriptures. Everyone left equipped and eager to read their Bible again. Mitch is a terrific communicator, and his knowledge of and passion for God and His self-revelation were clearly evident. I was encouraged, challenged, and refreshed by Mitch's presentation. I highly recommend *Clarifying the Bible.*"

—Beau Hughes,
Pastor, The Village Church Denton, Denton, TX

"Mitch's *Clarifying the Bible* presentation is terrific. He does a magnificent job. His survey of the Bible is compact, and the clarity is much needed. I found myself wishing I had had that as a young man. I didn't even get it in such a succinct package in seminary."

—Dr. Maxie Dunnam,
President Emeritus, Asbury Theological Seminary

"We don't need another Bible—we need more understanding of the one we already have. To me, this is the hallmark of *Clarifying the Bible*. The Bible can be a very daunting and intimidating book to most anyone. How can you possibly get your hands (and mind) around this massive work? What people need is a well-written, professional executive summary or overview. This is what we do in the business world. We start off reading these summaries to get a quick 'understanding of the offer, product, or situation.' If we elect to dig deeper for further clarification, we can refer to the details of the report. In a spiritual sense, this is what Mitch Maher has done. He has given us an executive overview of the Bible. *Clarifying the Bible* can help you comprehend and mentally grasp the big picture of the Bible. It is the 30,000-foot view. It leads and assists a person to have the intellectual capacity and stream of consciousness to follow this miraculous story. *Clarifying the Bible* has the potential to remove the scales from one's eyes and launch someone into a more profound relationship with the Bible and its teaching. Who could ask for more than this? It has made a big impact on my life. In my personal opinion, it is absolutely invaluable."

—Kem Wilson,
Vice Chairman, Board of Directors,
Kemmons Wilson Companies, Memphis, TN,
Board of Directors, Downline Ministries, Memphis, TN

"When someone asks, 'Where do I start in reading the Bible?' they are often told, 'Start by reading the book of John.' That's a great answer, but where do you go from there? I think *Clarifying the Bible*. This presentation gives a novice reader as well as a learned student a grasp of the overall contents of the Bible. Sure, I think it should be mandatory reading for junior high and high school students, but for seminary students as well. It's also perfect for Bible study classes at any church. Without trying to give 'his personal' interpretation of what the Bible says, Mitch Maher has tried to give a concise overview of its contents—all in less than two hours. It's much more than a table of contents—it's a solid look at what the Bible's all about."

–Dwight Morris,
Oral Surgeon, Memphis, TN

"Mitch Maher is a gifted teacher and communicator, mixed with incredible humility. Mitch is passionate about teaching the Bible all the way from Genesis to Revelation. He has an incredible ability to take very academic information and make it very practical to your life. Mitch has been an instrumental part of the Kanakuk Institute, which takes the cream of the crop of approximately 60 college graduates per year from a staff of over 2,500 from Kanakuk Kamps and equips them with biblical skills for a lifetime of ministry. The information in *Clarifying the Bible* is an essential part of the spiritual development of any believer, no matter what the age. However, I strongly feel that this resource and Mitch's teaching would be greatly influential to any college or school setting."

–Keith Chancey,
President, Kanakuk Institute

CLARIFYING THE BIBLE

A MEDIA EXPERIENCE TO HELP MAKE SENSE OF IT ALL

MITCH MAHER

LUCIDBOOKS

DOWNLOAD YOUR VIDEOS NOW!

Congratulations! Your purchase of this book allows you to download the digital videos on my website for **FREE**. Please see code and instructions located at the back of this book and enjoy!

Table of Contents

Introduction

One of my favorite quotes about the Bible comes from an unknown author:

> This Book is the mind of God, the state of man, the way of salvation, the doom of sinners, and the happiness of believers. Its doctrines are holy, its precepts are binding; its histories are true, and its decisions are immutable. Read it to be wise, believe it to be safe, practice it to be holy. It contains light to direct you, food to support you, and comfort to cheer you. It is the traveler's map, the pilgrim's staff, the pilot's compass, the soldier's sword, and the Christian's character. Here paradise is restored, heaven opened, and the gates of hell disclosed. Christ is its grand subject, our good its design, and the glory of God its end. It should fill the memory, rule the heart, and guide the feet. Read it slowly, frequently, prayerfully. It is a mine of wealth, a paradise of glory, and a river of pleasure. Follow its precepts and it will lead you to Calvary, to the empty tomb, to a resurrected life in Christ; yes, to glory itself, for eternity.[1]

Wow! *Clarifying the Bible* is my effort to help you understand the big picture of the Bible with a view toward motivating you to a lifetime of personal devotion to the Scriptures. Originally produced in 2007, updated in 2013, and now given a new look in 2017, this resource has been used by God to bless thousands of lives. I'm very hopeful that this newest version helps a whole new generation dive into God's Word with greater confidence than ever before.

Special thanks are due to a number of people. Dr. Dwight Morris and Kem Wilson, Jr., both of Memphis, Tennessee, shared the original vision and passion that got this project off the ground years ago. Their guidance and support in the early days were unparalleled. The 2013 new and improved experience of *Clarifying the Bible* was greatly supported by Kem and Norma Wilson, David and Sharon Sheridan, Will and Vickie Hussey, Nathan and Tiffany Dagley, Ronnie and Kay Cotten, Steve and Cynthia Kragthorpe, and my parents, Bob and Jean Maher. John Carroll and his team at City Leadership in Memphis were awesome in guiding all the improvements to *Clarifying the Bible* at that time. Now, Casey Cease and the good folks at Lucid Books have given a fresh look to the book and website, and are helping take *Clarifying the Bible* to a new and growing audience. They have been wonderful to work with in recent months.

Finally, my wonderful wife, Tara, makes my life so much sweeter. Beyond the daily love and support she provides so faithfully, she has sat through my *Clarifying the Bible* presentation more than any other and always greets me with a big smile, a nice hug, and an encouraging word. She is a gift from God, along with our three girls—Macy, Molly, and Maddy—and life would not be the same without them.

May God use *Clarifying the Bible* to spur you on so that the Scriptures might fill your memory, rule your heart, and guide your feet.

Mitch Maher
November 2017
mitch@clarifyingthebible.com

How To Use This Workbook

This workbook is designed to complement and enhance your experience of *Clarifying the Bible*. In Section I, you'll find visual aids that accompany the presentation as well as additional space for note taking. Section II dives deeper into each of the 20 key sentences, offering you more information and further insight. Section II should be read, reread, and studied like a book. Section I, on the other hand, is best experienced in conjunction with the video presentation available on the website.

Experience
Use Section I the first time you experience *Clarifying the Bible*. You can watch in one sitting or section by section at your own pace.

Interact
As you watch the presentation, follow along and take notes in Section I. Write down key insights or lingering questions.

Study

Use Section II for further study. This section is packed with information and insights related to each portion of the presentation. It should be read, reread, and referenced when you need to review key concepts.

Share

Teach someone else what *Clarifying the Bible* has taught you! If you are teaching this material to a bigger group (such as a church or large Bible study), free PowerPoint slides are available to accompany your presentation.

Digital downloads and DVDs of *Clarifying the Bible* can be found at clarifyingthebible.com.

Section I:
Video Notes

1-4:
A Broad Overview of the
Entire Bible

1

The Bible is the...

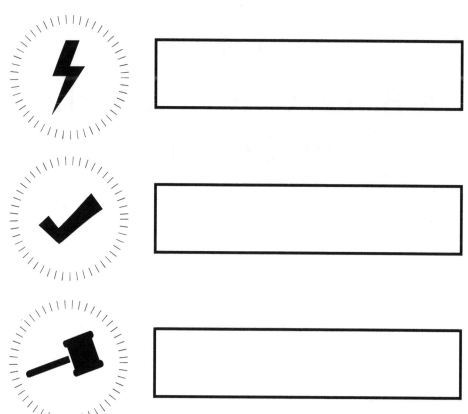

...word of God.

1

....
....
....
....
....
....
....
....
....
....
....
....
....
....
....
....
....
....
....
....
....
....
....
....
....
....

2

The Bible is _____ book

HOLY BIBLE

that consists of _____

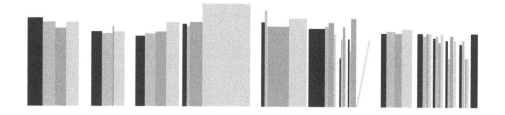

individual books.

2

....
....
....
....
....
....
....
....
....
....
....
....
....
....
....
....
....
....
....
....
....
....
....
....
....
....
....

3

The Bible's
_____ books
are divided
into _____
testaments.

&

the Old Testament with   the New Testament with

_____ books   _____ books

3

THE BIBLE

OLD TESTAMENT

Genesis
Exodus
Leviticus
Numbers
Deuteronomy
Joshua
Judges
Ruth
1 Samuel
2 Samuel
1 Kings
2 Kings
1 Chronicles
2 Chronicles
Ezra
Nehemiah
Esther

Job
Psalms
Proverbs
Ecclesiastes
Song of Solomon

Isaiah
Jeremiah
Lamentations
Ezekiel
Daniel
Hosea
Joel
Amos
Obadiah
Jonah
Micah
Nahum
Habakkuk
Zephaniah
Haggai
Zechariah
Malachi

NEW TESTAMENT

Matthew
Mark
Luke
John
Acts

Romans
1 Corinthians
2 Corinthians
Galatians
Ephesians
Philippians
Colossians
1 Thessalonians
2 Thessalonians
1 Timothy
2 Timothy
Titus
Philemon

Hebrews
James
1 Peter
2 Peter
1 John
2 John
3 John
Jude

Revelation

4

OLD

(Genesis – Malachi)

The big picture of the Bible can be understood in terms of five Christ-centered divisions.

NEW

(Matthew – John)

(Acts)

(Romans – Jude)

(Revelation)

4

....
....
....
....
....
....
....
....
....
....
....
....
....
....
....
....
....
....
....
....
....
....
....
....
....
....

5-12:
A Broad Overview of the
Old Testament

5

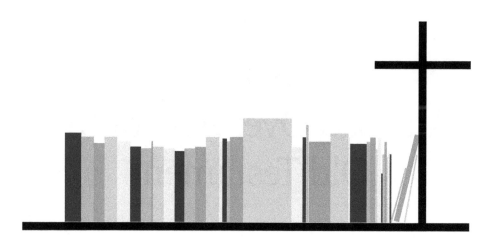

The Old Testament
consists of _____
books written _____
the birth of Jesus Christ.

5

....
....
....
....
....
....
....
....
....
....
....
....
....
....
....
....
....
....
....
....
....
....
....
....
....

6

The 39 books of
the Old Testament
are divided into

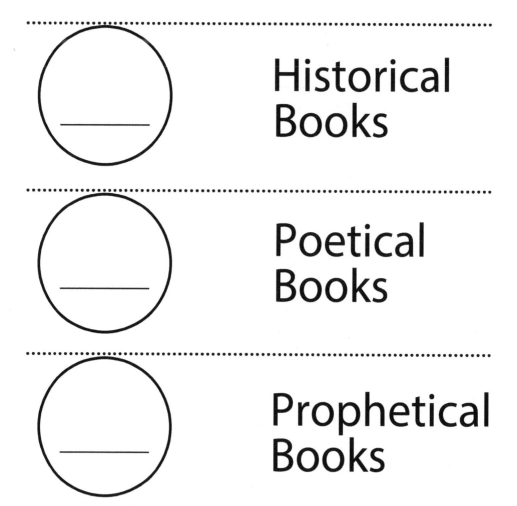

**Historical
Books**

**Poetical
Books**

**Prophetical
Books**

6

THE BOOKS OF THE OLD TESTAMENT

HISTORICAL BOOKS	POETICAL BOOKS	PROPHETICAL BOOKS
Genesis	Job	Isaiah
Exodus	Psalms	Jeremiah
Leviticus	Proverbs	Lamentations
Numbers	Ecclesiastes	Ezekiel
Deuteronomy	Song of Solomon	Daniel
Joshua		Hosea
Judges		Joel
Ruth		Amos
1 Samuel		Obadiah
2 Samuel		Jonah
1 Kings		Micah
2 Kings		Nahum
1 Chronicles		Habakkuk
2 Chronicles		Zephaniah
Ezra		Haggai
Nehemiah		Zechariah
Esther		Malachi

7

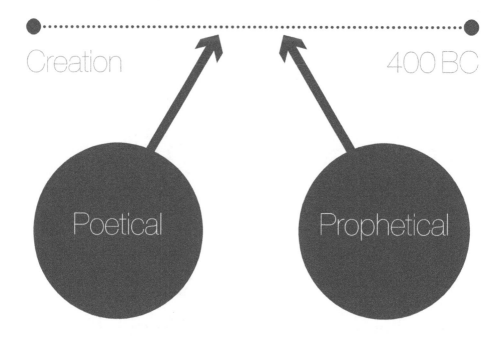

The key to understanding the Old Testament is to realize
that the Historical Books cover the _____
of the Old Testament from creation to approximately
400 BC, while the remaining Poetical and Prophetical
Books _____ at proper places within that story line.

7

8

The major story line of the Old
Testament can be understood by
following Max Anders's nine eras
of Old Testament history:[2]

_____

_____

_____

_____

_____

_____

_____

_____

_____

8

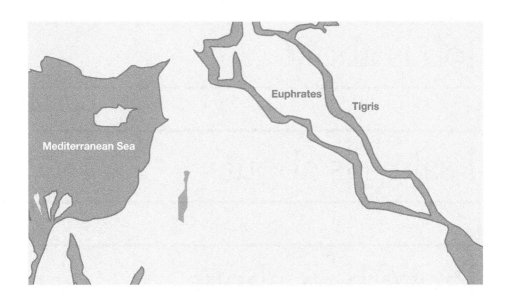

....
....
....
....
....
....
....
....
....
....
....
....
....

9

Concerning the
Poetical Books:

Job is about

```
┌─────────────────────────────────────┐
│                                       │
│                                       │
└─────────────────────────────────────┘
```

Psalms is about

```
┌─────────────────────────────────────┐
│                                       │
│                                       │
└─────────────────────────────────────┘
```

Proverbs is about

```
┌─────────────────────────────────────┐
│                                       │
│                                       │
└─────────────────────────────────────┘
```

Ecclesiastes is about

```
┌─────────────────────────────────────┐
│                                       │
│                                       │
└─────────────────────────────────────┘
```

Song of Solomon is about

```
┌─────────────────────────────────────┐
│                                       │
│                                       │
└─────────────────────────────────────┘
```

9

....
....
....
....
....
....
....
....
....
....
....
....
....
....
....
....
....
....
....
....
....
....
....
....
....
....
....
....
....

10

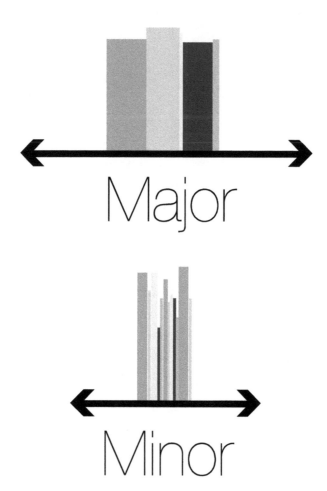

Major

Minor

Concerning the Prophetical Books, the first thing to know is that the descriptions Major and Minor refer to _____ and _____. (So, don't be misled.)

10

....
....
....
....
....
....
....
....
....
....
....
....
....
....
....
....
....
....
....
....
....
....
....
....
....

11

The second thing to know concerning the Prophetical Books is that there are three major categories,

_____   _____

_____   _____

though three Prophetical Books do not fit into these categories.

11

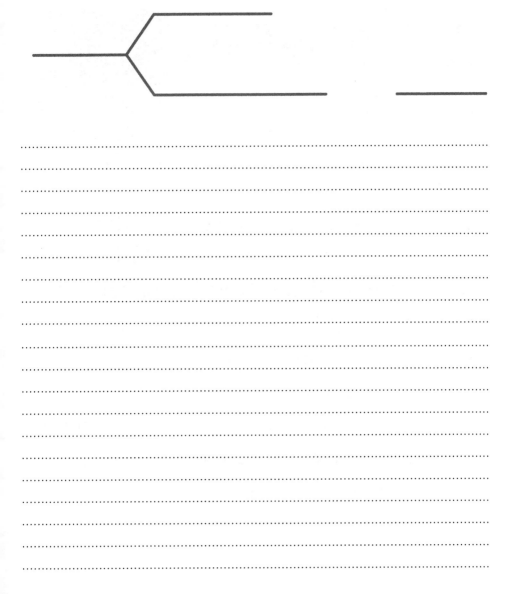

12

The period between the end of the Old Testament (approximately 400 BC) and the beginning of the New Testament (the ministry of John the Baptist around 30 AD) is often referred to as the _____ _____ because there was no prophetic word from God during this time, though God was at work behind the scenes preparing the way for His Son.

12

....

....

....

....

....

....

....

....

....

....

....

....

....

....

....

....

....

....

....

....

....

....

....

....

....

....

....

....

13-20:
A Broad Overview of the
New Testament

13

The New Testament consists of _____ books written by the early followers of Jesus Christ.

13

....
....
....
....
....
....
....
....
....
....
....
....
....
....
....
....
....
....
....
....
....
....
....
....
....

14

The 27 books
of the New
Testament are
divided into

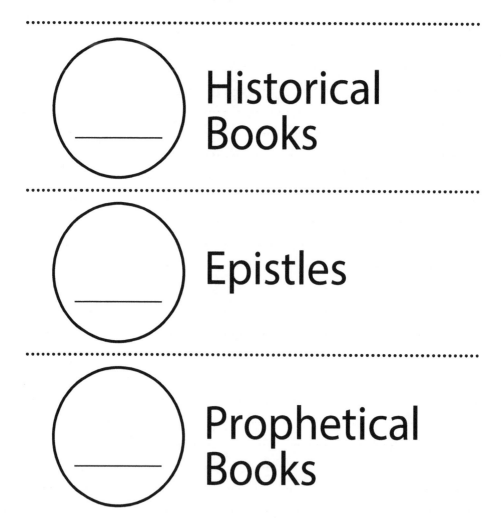

Historical
Books

Epistles

Prophetical
Books

14

....
....
....
....
....
....
....
....
....
....
....
....
....
....
....
....
....
....
....
....
....
....
....
....
....
....
....
....

15

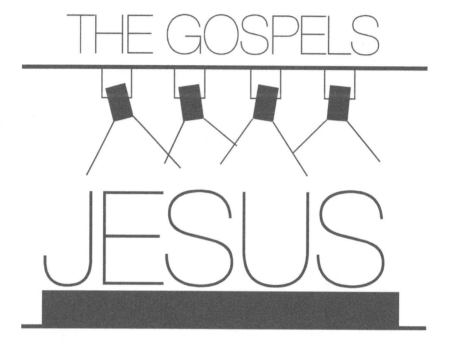

The Gospels present the life and ministry of Jesus Christ from the unique perspectives of four different _____ writing to four different _____ with four different _____ in mind, and together they illuminate the majesty of our Savior.

15

....
....
....
....
....
....
....
....
....
....
....
....
....
....
....
....
....
....
....
....
....
....
....
....
....

16

The book of Acts records the spread of the church from its birth (1:1–2:43) and expansion in _____ (3:1–6:7) to its extension into _____ (6:8–9:31), _____ (9:32–12:24), _____ (12:25–16:5), the _____ region (16:6–19:20), and _____ (19:21–28:31). Each movement is summarized with a progress report from Luke.

16

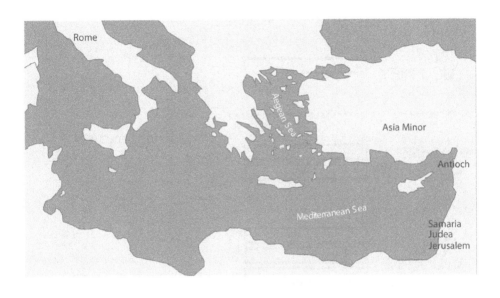

....
....
....
....
....
....
....
....
....
....
....
....
....
....

17

The Pauline Letters
are best understood in
their historical context:

1st*ℓℓ*
JOURNEY

2nd*ℓℓ*
JOURNEY

3rd*ℓℓ*
JOURNEY

Paul's Journeys

1st

Paul's Imprisonments
& Release

2nd

17

1st Missionary Journey

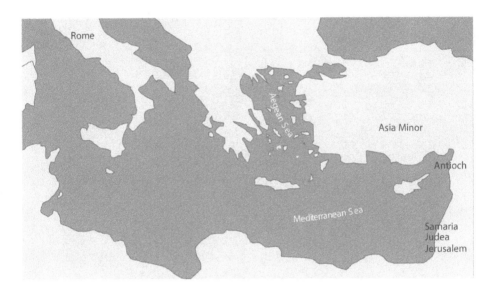

....
....
....
....
....
....
....
....
....
....
....
....
....

17

2nd Missionary Journey

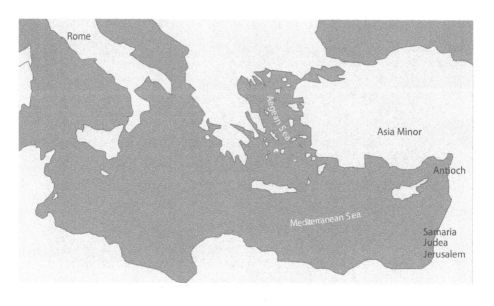

....
....
....
....
....
....
....
....
....
....
....
....
....

17

3rd Missionary Journey

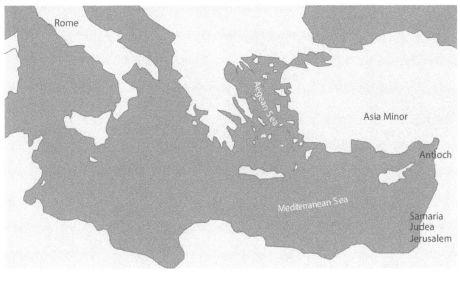

....

....

....

....

....

....

....

....

....

....

....

....

17

1st Roman Imprisonment

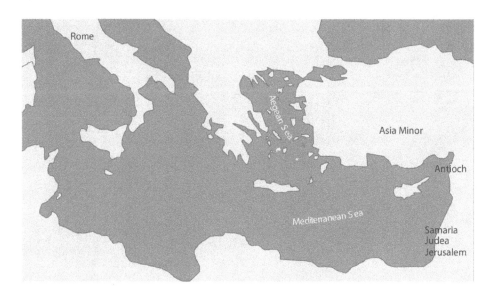

....
....
....
....
....
....
....
....
....
....
....

17

2nd Roman Imprisonment

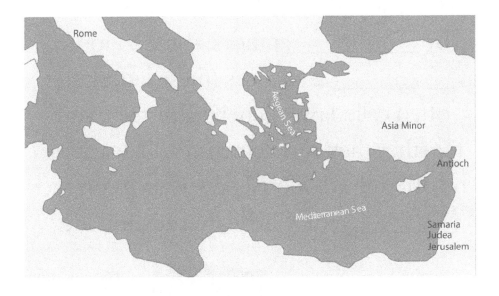

....
....
....
....
....
....
....
....
....
....
....
....

18

The Non-Pauline Letters were written by _____ authors, some to more _____ audiences (these letters are often called the General Epistles), and together they supplement Paul's teaching by offering additional perspectives on the _____ of Christian truth and life.[3]

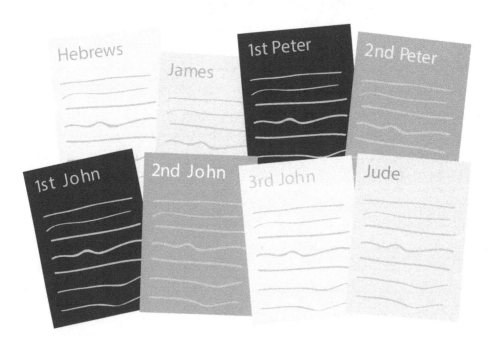

18

....
....
....
....
....
....
....
....
....
....
....
....
....
....
....
....
....
....
....
....
....
....
....
....
....
....

19

REVELATION

Bible and records the_____
John saw (1:12-16), Jesus's letters to
the_____ of John's day
(Ch. 2-3), and the things that will take
place in the _____ (Ch. 4-22), most
clearly the Second Coming of Jesus
Christ and the life everlasting for both
the saved and the unsaved.

19

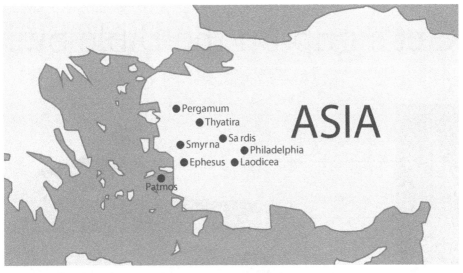

....

....

....

....

....

....

....

....

....

....

....

....

20

Get a grip on the Bible by...

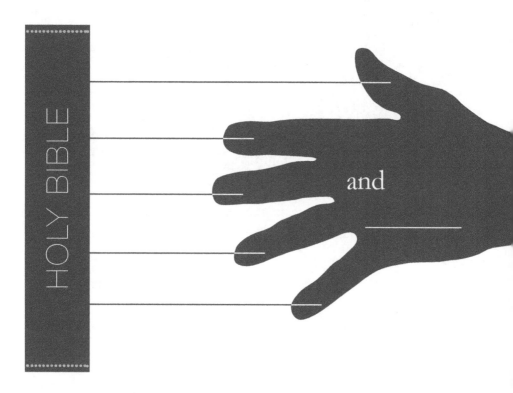

HOLY BIBLE

and

the Bible for a lifetime.

20

....
....
....
....
....
....
....
....
....
....
....
....
....
....
....
....
....
....
....
....
....
....
....
....

Section II:
Notes For
Further Study

57

1-4: A Broad Overview of The Entire Bible

1. The Bible is the <u>inspired</u>, <u>inerrant</u>, and <u>authoritative</u> word of God.

INSPIRED

"Inspiration is the act by which God superintended the human authors of the Bible so that they composed and recorded without error his message to mankind in the words of their original writings."[4]

2 Timothy 3:16–17

"All Scripture is inspired by God and profitable for teaching, for reproof, for correction, for training in righteousness; so that the man of God may be adequate, equipped for every good work."

2 Peter 1:20–21

"But know this first of all, that no prophecy of Scripture is a matter of one's own interpretation, for no prophecy was ever made by an act of human will, but men moved by the Holy Spirit spoke from God."

INERRANT

"Inerrancy means that when all facts are known the Scriptures in their original autographs and properly interpreted will be shown to be wholly true in everything that they affirm, whether that has to do with doctrine or morality or with the social, physical, or life sciences."[5]

Psalm 12:6

"The words of the Lord are pure words; As silver tried in a furnace on the earth, refined seven times."

AUTHORITATIVE

"The authority of Scripture means all the words in Scripture are God's words. To disbelieve or disobey any word of Scripture is to disbelieve or disobey God."[6]

2. The Bible is <u>1</u> book that consists of <u>66</u> individual books.

The Bible is one book. Its title, "The Bible," literally means "the book." However, it's made up of sixty-six individual books.

As one carefully considers the production of the Bible, taking note of its incredible unity despite its incredible diversity, it becomes evident that standing behind the multiple authors of these individual books is really only one Author of one book.

Consider the Bible's diversity:

The Bible was written over a period of fifteen hundred years.
Moses penned Genesis through Deuteronomy sometime around 1400 BC. The Apostle John penned Revelation sometime around 90 AD.

The Bible was written by over forty different authors from various walks of life.
Moses was a political statesman, David a shepherd, Solomon a king, Amos a fig-picker, Matthew a tax-collector, Luke a physician, Paul a rabbi, and Peter a fisherman.

The Bible was written in three different languages.
Most of the Old Testament was written in Hebrew, though some small portions were written in Aramaic. The New Testament was written in Greek.

The Bible was written on three different continents.
Different books of the Bible were written in Africa, Asia, and Europe.

The Bible was written in various moods.
David wrote many of his Psalms from the depths of sorrow as he fled for his life, while Solomon no doubt penned much of his work from the comfortable quarters of his kingly palace.

The Bible was written in various locations.
Moses wrote in the wilderness, David sometimes in a cave, Paul often from prison, Luke possibly on a boat, and John on the island of Patmos.[7]

Yet, amid all of that incredible diversity, from Genesis to Revelation the Bible demonstrates an extraordinary unity. That leads to the conclusion that behind the multiple human authors of multiple books of Scripture, the Bible is one Book with one Author!

3. The Bible's 66 books are divided into 2 testaments: the Old Testament with 39 books and the New Testament with 27 books.

THE BOOKS OF THE OLD TESTAMENT		
HISTORICAL BOOKS	POETICAL BOOKS	PROPHETICAL BOOKS
Genesis	Job	Isaiah
Exodus	Psalms	Jeremiah
Leviticus	Proverbs	Lamentations
Numbers	Ecclesiastes	Ezekiel
Deuteronomy	Song of Solomon	Daniel
Joshua		Hosea
Judges		Joel
Ruth		Amos
1 Samuel		Obadiah
2 Samuel		Jonah
1 Kings		Micah
2 Kings		Nahum
1 Chronicles		Habakkuk
2 Chronicles		Zephaniah
Ezra		Haggai
Nehemiah		Zechariah
Esther		Malachi

4. The big picture of the Bible can be understood in terms of five Christ-centered divisions: anticipation (Genesis–Malachi), manifestation (Matthew–John), proclamation (Acts), explanation (Romans–Jude), and consummation (Revelation).

The entire Bible—including those books written before His birth—is all about Jesus!

ANTICIPATION (Genesis–Malachi): The entire Old Testament is the anticipation of the coming of Jesus Christ. It has been said, "If you sat down and read through the entire Old Testament, a recurring theme would come to the surface: 'Someone's coming . . . Someone's coming . . . Someone's coming.'" The Old Testament contains prophecies only He will fulfill and problems only He will fix. It speaks of people who prefigure His coming and pictures that foreshadow His work. The Old Testament anticipates Jesus!

MANIFESTATION (Matthew–John): The One who was anticipated throughout the Old Testament is manifested in the Gospels. "Someone's coming . . . Someone's coming . . . Someone's coming . . . He's here!" A reading of the Gospels quickly shows that they record the birth, life, teaching, miracles, death, burial, and resurrection of Jesus Christ. The Gospels manifest Jesus!

PROCLAMATION (Acts): The One who was anticipated throughout the Old Testament and manifested in the Gospels is proclaimed in the book of Acts. This book traces the growth of the early church and the proclamation of the gospel of Jesus Christ from the city of Jerusalem in Acts 1:1–6:7, to the surrounding regions of Judea and Samaria in Acts 6:8–9:31, to Antioch in Acts 9:32–12:24, to Asia Minor in Acts 12:25–16:5, to the regions surrounding the Aegean Sea in Acts 16:6–19:20, and finally to Rome in Acts 19:21–28:31. In the book of Acts, the early church proclaims Jesus!

EXPLANATION (Romans–Jude): The One who was anticipated throughout the Old Testament, manifested in the Gospels, and proclaimed in the book of Acts is explained in the epistles, Romans to Jude. These books (properly understood as letters, or to use the fancy word, *epistles*) were written to both churches and individuals, addressing pertinent needs, problems, and questions. But, from a big-picture perspective, these letters explain who Jesus Christ is, what He accomplished (especially on the cross), and how His followers should live in light of those truths. The epistles explain the person and work of Jesus!

CONSUMMATION (Revelation): Finally, the One who was anticipated throughout the Old Testament, manifested in the Gospels, proclaimed in the book of Acts, and explained in the epistles, is the One in whom all of God's purposes for history will be consummated. To consummate means, "to finish." What God started in Genesis, He will finish in the book of Revelation. As it is written, "The kingdom of the world has become the kingdom of our Lord and of His Christ; and He will reign forever and ever" (Revelation 11:15). The Lord Jesus will return, the wicked will be judged, and the righteous will be blessed forevermore. The book of Revelation consummates all of history in Jesus!

5-12: A Broad Overview Of The Old Testament

5. The Old Testament consists of <u>39</u> books written <u>before</u> the birth of Jesus Christ.

The Bible is divided into an Old Testament of thirty-nine books and a New Testament of twenty-seven books. Now, the important thing to know is that the thirty-nine books of the Old Testament were written before the birth of Jesus Christ.

Remember, the Old Testament anticipates the coming of Jesus Christ, so it becomes obvious that these were written before His birth.

6. The 39 books of the Old Testament are divided into <u>17</u> Historical Books, <u>5</u> Poetical Books, and <u>17</u> Prophetical Books.

THE BOOKS OF THE OLD TESTAMENT		
HISTORICAL BOOKS	POETICAL BOOKS	PROPHETICAL BOOKS
Genesis	Job	Isaiah
Exodus	Psalms	Jeremiah
Leviticus	Proverbs	Lamentations
Numbers	Ecclesiastes	Ezekiel
Deuteronomy	Song of Solomon	Daniel
Joshua		Hosea
Judges		Joel
Ruth		Amos
1 Samuel		Obadiah
2 Samuel		Jonah
1 Kings		Micah
2 Kings		Nahum
1 Chronicles		Habakkuk
2 Chronicles		Zephaniah
Ezra		Haggai
Nehemiah		Zechariah
Esther		Malachi

In the Old Testament, there are three types of books—books of History, Poetry, and Prophecy. The first seventeen are the books of History; the next five are the books of Poetry, and the final seventeen are the books of Prophecy.

The seventeen Historical Books and the seventeen Prophetical Books are often broken up into two groups. That is because the first five books of the Bible (Genesis–Deuteronomy) were written by Moses and are often lumped together under names such as the Pentateuch, the Law, the Torah, or the Law of Moses. Therefore, they are sometimes set apart from the other twelve Historical Books (Joshua–Esther).

And the seventeen Prophetical Books are often broken up into two groups, the Major Prophets (Isaiah–Daniel) and the Minor Prophets (Hosea–Malachi).

So, the easiest way to think about the Old Testament is seventeen, five, seventeen: seventeen Historical Books, five Poetical Books, and seventeen Prophetical Books. But, it is also accurate to think five, twelve, five, five, twelve: five books of the Law, twelve Historical Books, five Poetical Books, five Major Prophets, and twelve Minor Prophets.

7. The key to understanding the Old Testament is to realize that the Historical Books cover the <u>major story line</u> of the Old Testament from creation to approximately 400 BC, while the remaining Poetical and Prophetical Books <u>fit in</u> at proper places within that story line.

It is easy to look at the thirty-nine books of the Old Testament and think those thirty-nine books recount the history of Israel, one book after another, starting in Genesis and ending with Malachi. But that is not the case.

THE HISTORICAL BOOKS
Genesis through Esther cover the major story line of the Old Testament—from the creation of the universe in Genesis to Nehemiah, approximately four hundred years before the birth of Jesus Christ. (Technically, the chronology of Esther fits into the chronology of Ezra, but don't worry about that right now!)

THE POETICAL BOOKS
Job through Song of Solomon fit in their proper places. For instance, the book of Job tells the story of a man who lived during the time of Abraham, Isaac, or Jacob

(Genesis). David wrote many of the Psalms. His life is found in 1 and 2 Samuel, so the Psalms that he wrote fit in at that time. Or take Solomon, who wrote many of the Proverbs along with Ecclesiastes and the Song of Solomon. His life is recorded in 1 Kings 1-11, so all of these writings fit in during that time period.

THE PROPHETICAL BOOKS

Isaiah through Malachi fit in later in the story of Israel's history (1 and 2 Kings, Ezra, and Nehemiah), for the most part pre-exilic, exilic, or post-exilic. That will make sense later in the presentation.

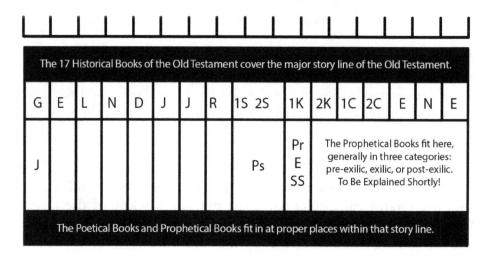

8. The major story line of the Old Testament can be understood by following Max Anders's nine eras of Old Testament history: Creation, Patriarch, Exodus, Conquest, Judges, Kingdom, Exile, Return, and Silence.[8]

In his book *30 Days to Understanding the Bible*, Max Anders makes this story line more easily grasped. He divides Old Testament history into nine "eras" that summarize the story told in Genesis through Esther, the seventeen Historical Books of the Old Testament.

Anders summarizes the Historical Books using the following eras:

CREATION

The Old Testament begins when God created Adam and Eve in a perfect paradise. They later sinned and were driven out of the Garden of Eden, forced to live "by the sweat of their brow" in an imperfect world. As their offspring multiplied, sin also multiplied. Eventually, humanity became so sinful that, as judgment, God destroyed the earth with a universal flood, preserving only Noah and his immediate family on the ark to repopulate the earth.

PATRIARCH

Sin kept its hold over humanity, however, and once again people forgot God. As the years passed, God revealed Himself to Abraham (two thousand years before Christ), promising him a nation, many descendants, and a blessing that would ultimately extend to everyone on the earth. Abraham believed God and became the father of the Hebrew people. Abraham had a son, Isaac, and Isaac had a son, Jacob. The promises God made to Abraham were passed down through Isaac and Jacob. Jacob had twelve sons, and the promises were passed to all twelve sons, who became the fathers of the twelve tribes of Israel.

EXODUS

Jacob and his family of about seventy people were living in the land of Canaan when a famine hit. They were forced to migrate to Egypt to get food. In time, they became so numerous that they were perceived as a threat by the Egyptian people, and the Egyptians enslaved the Hebrew people for nearly four hundred years. Finally (approximately fifteen hundred years before Christ), God raised up Moses to lead them out of Egypt with many astounding miracles, including the crossing of the Red Sea. They escaped Egypt and went to Mount Sinai, where they received the Ten Commandments. Then they rebelled against God again and, as a judgment, wandered in the wilderness for forty years.

CONQUEST

When their time of judgment was up, they were allowed to enter the Promised Land. Moses died, and Joshua led in the conquest of the land.

JUDGES

Israel lived in the Promised Land in a loose governmental system, ruled by judges, for the next four hundred years. Samson and Samuel were the most famous judges.

KINGDOM

Then Israel insisted on establishing a monarchy (approximately one thousand years before Christ), and the Hebrews were ruled by kings for the next four hundred years. Saul, David, and Solomon were the first three kings, who ruled over a united monarchy for one hundred and twenty years (forty years each). When Solomon died, the nation divided over the issue of taxation. There was now a northern kingdom, which kept the name Israel, because a majority (ten) of the tribes were loyal to the north, and the southern kingdom, which was called Judah, because Judah was by far the larger of the two southern tribes.

EXILE

Because of the accumulating sin of Israel, Assyria, a nation to the northeast, came and conquered Israel and scattered many of the people throughout that part of the world. About one hundred fifty years later, because of the accumulating sin of Judah, Babylonia came and conquered Judah, destroyed Jerusalem, and took many of the people into captivity in Babylonia.

RETURN

About seventy years later, Persia defeated Babylonia, who had previously defeated Assyria. Thus, Persia now ruled the entire part of the world from the eastern shores of the Mediterranean Sea to the borders of India. The king of Persia allowed the Israelites living in captivity in Babylonia to return to Jerusalem to rebuild it. Fifty thousand people returned (approximately five hundred years before Christ), rebuilt the city, rebuilt the temple, and restored ceremonial worship of God.

SILENCE

They continued to live that way for the next four hundred years. During that time, Persia fell to Greece, and Greece in turn fell to Rome. Rome was ruling that part of the world when Jesus was born.

Summaries of the 17 Historical Books

Building upon Anders's summary, I created the following summaries of each of the seventeen Historical Books.

GENESIS

The book of Genesis records the early events of world history and the beginning of God's work of redemption through Abraham and his family. The first twelve chapters record God's work of creation, mankind's fall into sin, the judgment of the flood, and the rebellion at the tower of Babel. The remaining chapters tell of God's dealing with the patriarchs—Abraham, Isaac, Jacob, and Joseph. At the end of Genesis, Jacob's family, his twelve sons, and his sons' families have migrated to Egypt.

EXODUS

The book of Exodus records the deliverance of God's people from Egyptian slavery and their journey to Mount Sinai where they enter into covenant with God. The first part of Exodus records the family's incredible growth in Egypt, hardship under Egypt's new pharaoh, cry to God for help, and deliverance through Moses's leadership. Moses delivered God's people through ten plagues, culminating in the Passover. The book then records the crossing of the Red Sea and the Israelites' journey to Mount Sinai where God entered into the Mosaic Covenant with His people. At Sinai, God revealed the Ten Commandments and instructions for constructing the tabernacle. The book closes with the completion of the tabernacle and its filling with the glory of God.

LEVITICUS

Leviticus records God's further instructions for His people that He revealed at Mount Sinai. These instructions concerned how His people should approach and obey Him. They took up matters related to sacrifices; the priesthood; the clean and unclean; the day of atonement; social, civil, and ceremonial law; the heart of the Mosaic Law (the blessings and curses); and vows.

NUMBERS

Numbers records the people's departure from Mount Sinai, wanderings in the wilderness, and arrival at the plains of Moab on the east side of the Jordan River. After numbering their men of war and organizing around the tabernacle, Israel's twelve tribes set out from Sinai headed toward the Promised Land. At Kadesh-Barnea, a city south of the land, they sent twelve spies to survey the land. The spies returned; ten gave a fearful report, and the people believed the fearful spies. Because of this, God judged the people; the nation spent forty years in the wilderness, and everyone over twenty years old died, except Caleb and Joshua. After the old generation died, a new generation arose and made their way to the east side of the Jordan River, poised to enter the Promised Land.

DEUTERONOMY

Deuteronomy records Moses's final words to the young generation. Having committed a sin that would keep him from the Promised Land (Numbers 20), Moses addressed the new generation that was about to possess it. He pointed them to the past, warning of disobedience. He encouraged them in the present, calling for obedience. He looked ahead, foreseeing Israel's future dispersion to the nations but ultimate return. Moses then died on Mount Nebo.

JOSHUA

The book of Joshua recounts Israel's successful conquest of the Promised Land. Joshua took Moses's place as the new leader of the people. They crossed the Jordan River, toppled Jericho, and defeated Canaanite enemies in the central, southern, and northern portions of the land. After completing the initial conquest, the nation divided the land among the twelve tribes, designated cities of refuge, and set apart forty-eight cities for the Levites. Finally, before his death, Joshua addressed the people and encouraged them to fear and serve the Lord.

JUDGES

The book of Judges records Israel's three hundred plus years of disobedience to God and the resulting hardship it brought. Having disobeyed the Lord's commands to utterly destroy the Canaanites, to avoid intermarriage, and to reject idolatry (Deuteronomy 7:1–5), the nation plunged into numerous cycles of sin, servitude, supplication, and salvation. Israel sinned against God. The Lord raised up a foreign nation to which Israel suffered servitude for years. The nation prayed to God for deliverance. (*Supplication* is a fancy word for prayer.) The Lord called a judge to save His people and bring peace. After that particular judge died, the cycle started all over again—time and time again. This book ends with an intense look at the idolatry and immorality that marked God's people during this age.

RUTH

The book of Ruth records the story of a Moabite woman, Ruth, who married an Israelite man, Boaz, and became a progenitor of David, the eventual king of the nation. The events of this book do not further the story line of the Old Testament, but rather take place during the time of the judges. In contrast to the darkness of that period, Ruth was a shining light—a Moabite woman who demonstrated the faith, love, and righteousness that were so lacking in Israel.

1 SAMUEL

The book of 1 Samuel records Israel's transition from a loose federation of twelve tribes to the united kingdom of Israel under their first king, Saul. After centuries under judges, Israel cried out for a king. God used Samuel, Israel's last judge, to anoint Israel's first king, Saul, in 1051 BC. Though he brought stability to the nation, Saul served without a passion for God. His disobedience was evident, and his insecurity was displayed in his attempts to kill young David, a faithful servant in the king's court. Saul's life ended in shame as he fell upon his own sword in an act of suicide.

2 SAMUEL

Originally one book with 1 Samuel, 2 Samuel records the rise of David to the throne of Israel, along with the painful consequences his sins brought into his life. After Saul's death, David became king in 1011 BC. The initial years of his rule were marked by great triumph as he established his rule over all Israel, founded Jerusalem as the capital of the nation, returned the Ark of the Covenant to Jerusalem, and won many victories over Israel's enemies. But his kingship took a troubled turn through his acts of adultery and murder, his son Amnon's rape of his half-sister, and his son Absalom's estrangement and attempted coup against his father.

1 KINGS

The book of 1 Kings records Solomon's reign over Israel before recording the division of the kingdom. After David's death, Solomon became king in 971 BC. His reign was marked by remarkable success as he excelled in wisdom, wealth, and accomplishment in the building and dedication of the temple in Jerusalem. But Solomon's multiple marriages to foreign women turned his heart from the Lord. A reign that started so strong ended in a whimper. At Solomon's death the kingdom of Israel split into the northern kingdom of Israel (ten tribes) and the southern kingdom of Judah (two tribes) in 931 BC. The histories of the two kingdoms follow and are carried on in the book of 2 Kings.

2 KINGS

The book of 2 Kings begins where 1 Kings left off (originally, these were one book), recounting the history of the two kingdoms—Israel, the northern kingdom, and Judah, the southern kingdom. The northern kingdom of Israel's rebellion against God eventually brought judgment when the Assyrians defeated and deported them out of their land. This is recorded in 2 Kings 17 and took place in 722 BC. The southern kingdom survived longer, being represented by some godly leadership, but eventually, the people's sin led to its demise. The Babylonians attacked Judah in 605 BC and 597 BC and finally destroyed the temple in Jerusalem in 586 BC, exporting the people of Judah to Babylon on all three occasions. These events are recorded in 2 Kings 25.

1 AND 2 CHRONICLES
Originally one book, 1 and 2 Chronicles do not further the story of the Old Testament, but rather cover much of the same history recorded in 2 Samuel, 1 Kings, and 2 Kings. These books were written after the return of the southern kingdom from Babylonian exile (see Ezra and Nehemiah) when the people were greatly discouraged. They had no king; the rebuilt temple lacked the glory of Solomon's former temple, and they were under the thumb of Persia. These books sought to encourage Judah by pointing to their storied past and God's faithfulness to bring them back to their land. (Remember, the Chronicles were written after Judah had returned to their land.)

EZRA
The book of Ezra records the return of Judah to their land, the rebuilding of the temple, and the ministry of Ezra. In fulfillment of His promise through Jeremiah to bring Judah back to their land after seventy years of captivity, God stirred up the heart of King Cyrus of Persia to allow the Jews to return to their land. Under Zerubbabel's leadership, fifty thousand Jews returned to the land and laid the foundation of the temple in 536 BC. They put off the work for sixteen years; then at the encouragement of the prophets Haggai and Zechariah, they finished the temple in 516 BC. In 457 BC, Ezra led two thousand others back to the land. With the word of God and prayer, Ezra led the people in repentance toward God.

NEHEMIAH
The book of Nehemiah records the return of Nehemiah and his successful effort to rebuild the walls around Jerusalem. Nehemiah served as the cupbearer to the Persian king Artaxerxes. After hearing the walls in Jerusalem remained in ruins, Nehemiah prayed God would give him an opportunity to return and rebuild the walls. After receiving permission from the king, Nehemiah returned, rallied the people, persevered through trials, and led the people to complete the rebuilding project in fifty-two days. The latter chapters record the further ministry of Ezra as

well as Nehemiah's own spiritual leadership.

ESTHER

The book of Esther records God's providential care for His people through a young Jewish girl named Esther who became queen of Persia. Chronologically, the book of Esther fits between Ezra 6 and Ezra 7, the book's events taking place from 483-473 BC. Though the name of God is not mentioned, His hand is evident throughout this book. When a decree was issued for the destruction of all Jews throughout the Persian Empire, a young Jewish girl named Esther was providentially in place to change their fate. Rather than being exterminated, the Jews were able to defend themselves and survive. The events of this story form the background of the feast of Purim, a feast still celebrated by Jews today.

9. Concerning the Poetical Books: Job is about <u>suffering</u>, Psalms is about <u>worship</u>, Proverbs is about <u>wisdom</u>, Ecclesiastes is about <u>meaning</u>, and Song of Solomon is about <u>marital romance</u>.

Remember, these five books do not further the story line of the Old Testament's history. Instead, they fit in according to when the author lived, or in the case of Job, when the character possibly lived.

The 17 Historical Books of the Old Testament cover the major story line of the Old Testament.															
G	E	L	N	D	J	J	R	1S 2S	1K	2K	1C	2C	E	N	E
J								Ps	Pr E SS	The Prophetical Books fit here, generally in three categories: pre-exilic, exilic, or post-exilic. To Be Explained Shortly!					
The Poetical Books and Prophetical Books fit in at proper places within that story line.															

JOB

The book of Job records the suffering and consequent shaping of a man named Job. This man suffered much—the loss of his wealth, his children, and his health. After receiving counsel from his wife and three friends, Job finally heard from God. Rather than giving Job the answers he was looking for, God pelted Job with a long series of questions designed to establish His sovereignty over all of life. Job responded well and submitted to his wise, powerful, and loving God.

PSALMS

The book of Psalms is a collection of poetical songs spanning nearly nine centuries of Israel's history used for both personal and corporate worship. The book is divided into five smaller books, Psalm 1–41, Psalm 42–72, Psalm 73–89, Psalm 90–106, and Psalm 107–150, each of which ends with a doxology. Plunging into the depths of human emotion, these psalms reflect the wide range of experience as one walks with God. Their intention is to capture readers' hearts and lift them to praise and worship the Lord.

PROVERBS

The book of Proverbs is a collection of sayings designed to give readers wisdom. They are arranged in poetic paragraphs in chapters 1–9; short, pithy maxims in chapters 10–29; and then paragraphs again in chapters 30–31. These proverbs address issues related to friendships, work, finances, sexuality, family, laziness, anger, the words one speaks, and so much more. They clearly set forth the consequences of both foolish and wise behavior.

ECCLESIASTES

The book of Ecclesiastes is Solomon's summary thoughts on man's search for meaning in life. Recounting his own personal quest, he said the deepest longings of his soul were not found in life without God—learning without God, money without God, or pleasure without God. No, true meaning and lasting joy can only be found by viewing life as a gift from the Creator and by living in obedience to Him. Life with God does not mean all life's mysteries will be understood, but that humble trust and simple submission are the path to a satisfied soul.

SONG OF SOLOMON

The Song of Solomon is a collection of love poems celebrating marital love and romance. In this book, through beautiful, picturesque language, the romantic love between man and woman finds full expression. The various poems celebrate the couple spending lingering time together, praising each other's beauty, expressing their mutual desire, and even consummating their love. The book is a clear reminder that God created romance and wants His children to enjoy it fully in the context of marriage.

10. Concerning the Prophetical Books, the first thing to know is that the descriptions "Major" and "Minor" refer to <u>length</u> and <u>not importance</u>. (So, don't be misled.)

The seventeen Prophetical Books are often split into two groups: the Major Prophets and the Minor Prophets.

This distinction has nothing to do with the importance or significance of the content of each book—it simply has to do with length. Isaiah has sixty-six chapters, Jeremiah has fifty-two, and Ezekiel has forty-eight—all Major Prophets; none of the Minor Prophets are longer than fourteen chapters. So, it is understandable why the distinction is often made. But the distinction is a bit inconsistent. Daniel, a Major Prophet, has only twelve chapters. Lamentations, another Major Prophet, has only five chapters. But Zechariah, a Minor Prophet, has fourteen chapters.

The point? Do not be surprised when the distinction is made between Major and Minor Prophets, but do not make the mistake of thinking the Major are more important than the Minor!

11. The second thing to know about the Prophetical Books is that there are three major categories: <u>pre-exilic</u>, <u>exilic</u>, and <u>post-exilic</u>, though three Prophetical Books do not fit into these categories.

After the period of the Judges, the nation of Israel desired a king. God established the monarchy in Israel as Saul became king in 1051 BC (1 Samuel 9). He reigned for forty years, and then David became king in 1011 BC (2 Samuel 2). After David reigned for forty years, his son Solomon became king in 971 BC (1 Kings 1).

Finally, Solomon reigned forty years, and after his death the nation split into the northern kingdom of Israel and the southern kingdom of Judah in 931 BC (1 Kings 12).

As time passed after this split, both Israel and Judah rebelled against the Lord. God sent prophets to His people, some to Israel in the north and some to Judah in the south, calling them back to obedience to His word and warning them of impending judgment if they continued to rebel. Thus, some of the prophets are understood as <u>pre-exilic</u>, i.e., they prophesied to either the northern or southern kingdom before that kingdom went into exile. Remember, the northern kingdom of Israel did not repent and was taken into captivity by the Assyrians in 722 BC. The northern kingdom never truly returned to the land. The southern kingdom of Judah held on a bit longer but was eventually taken into captivity by the Babylonians in 586 BC. They were allowed to return to their land at the decree of King Cyrus of Persia in 539 BC. Some of the prophets ministered while the southern kingdom was in captivity in Babylon and others ministered after they returned to the land; therefore, they are considered <u>exilic</u> and <u>post-exilic</u> prophets.

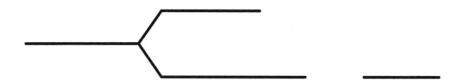

The split of the kingdom took place in 931 BC (1 Kings 12). The destruction of Israel (the northern kingdom) took place in 722 BC (2 Kings 17). The destruction of Judah (the southern kingdom) took place in 586 BC (2 Kings 25). Therefore, the prophets who ministered to Israel before that kingdom went into exile fit into the Old Testament's history before 2 Kings 17. Those who ministered to Judah before that kingdom went into exile fit into the history of the Old Testament before 2 Kings 25.

Again, after the northern kingdom of Israel went into exile, they never really returned to their land. Therefore, the Bible does not contain any prophets who ministered to them during or after their exile. Three prophets ministered to the southern kingdom during the exile, and three more ministered after the southern kingdom returned to their land.

		Pre-Exilic Prophets	_Exile_	Exilic Prophets	_Return_	Post Exilic Prophets
Kingdom split in 931 BC 1 Kings 12	To Israel (Northern Kingdom)	Amos Hosea	722 BC 2 Kings 17			
	To Judah (Southern Kingdom)	Joel Isaiah Micah Zephaniah Habakkuk Jeremiah	586 BC 2 Kings 25	Lamentations Ezekiel Daniel	539 BC Ezra 1-2	Haggai Zechariah Malachi

There are three Prophetical Books that do not fit into this chart—Obadiah, Jonah, and Nahum.

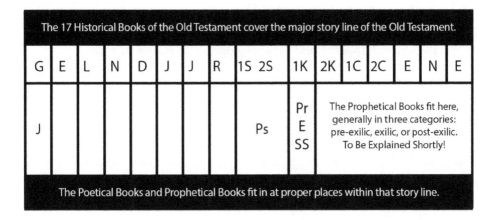

The 17 Historical Books of the Old Testament cover the major story line of the Old Testament.

G	E	L	N	D	J	J	R	1S 2S	1K	2K	1C	2C	E	N	E

J ... Ps ... Pr E SS

The Prophetical Books fit here, generally in three categories: pre-exilic, exilic, or post-exilic. To Be Explained Shortly!

The Poetical Books and Prophetical Books fit in at proper places within that story line.

To the Northern Kingdom of Israel before exile to Assyria in 722 BC

AMOS

God called Amos to prophesy against the northern kingdom of Israel prior to their exile to Assyria in 722 BC. After pronouncing judgment on the enemies of Israel, Amos stung the nation with a pronouncement against Israel itself. Because of their sins of dishonesty and oppression against the poor, empty religion, and pompous self-confidence, the nation was doomed to fall to the Assyrians. Like other prophets, though, Amos concluded his work with a word of consolation that God would restore Israel to glory and strength.

HOSEA

God's faithful love for His people Israel found clear illustration as God led the prophet Hosea to restore and welcome back his unfaithful wife Gomer. Hosea recounted Israel's sins against the Lord who had been so gracious and good. He also pronounced the coming judgment upon the nation through the one with whom unwise alliance had been made, Assyria. Despite Israel's rebellion and approaching judgment, the book closes with a word of hope that God will one day restore His people.

To the Southern Kingdom of Judah before exile to Babylon in 586 BC

JOEL

The prophet Joel looked to a recent locust plague as a foretaste of the judgment God would bring upon the southern kingdom of Judah in the Day of the Lord. After calling the people to repentance and warning of impending judgment, Joel prophesied of a future time when a remnant would repent, and God would restore the physical, spiritual, and national glory of the people of God.

ISAIAH

Isaiah prophesied chiefly to the southern kingdom of Judah prior to their exile to Babylon in 586 BC. The first part of this book, chapters 1-39, is filled with messages of judgment against both the nations and Judah. The last part of the book, chapters 40-66, is filled with messages of consolation for Judah as God promised to end their captivity, send their Messiah, and restore their nation to glory.

MICAH

While giving some attention to the northern kingdom of Israel, the primary recipient of Micah's ministry was the southern kingdom of Judah. He denounced this kingdom for their rebellion against the Lord, noting their outward formalism did not hide their inward corruption. Through a series of oracles, the prophet focused on the kingdom's sins, their coming judgment, and the Lord's ultimate restoration of those who repent.

ZEPHANIAH

Zephaniah ministered to the southern kingdom of Judah and focused on the coming Day of the Lord—a day of judgment and wrath against the Lord's sinful people. Yet the prophet proclaimed that a time would come when the fortunes of Judah would be restored through the faithfulness of their God.

HABAKKUK

The righteous prophet Habakkuk called out to the Lord to judge His sinful people, the southern kingdom of Judah, only to learn God would do so through the godless Babylonians. Shaken by this news—that God would use the wicked to judge those more righteous than they—the prophet appealed to God to consider the unrighteousness of the Babylonians. God replied that after using the Babylonians to judge His people, He would faithfully judge the Babylonians as well. The book closes with a strong affirmation of faith in the Lord.

JEREMIAH

Jeremiah prophesied chiefly to the southern kingdom of Judah prior to their exile to Babylon in 586 BC. Though Jeremiah was faithful to call God's people to repentance and warn them of impending judgment for their refusal to turn back to God, his work was met with resistance and rejection. Eventually his prophecies came true as the Babylonians took Judah captive. Jeremiah, often referred to as the "weeping prophet," watched lamentably the fall of the kingdom and destruction of their temple.

To the Southern Kingdom during their exile to Babylon in 586 BC

LAMENTATIONS

Lamentations, composed by the prophet Jeremiah, was written just after the destruction of Jerusalem's temple in 586 BC. Five laments spread over the book's five chapters. Each describes the prophet's anguish over the fallen kingdom and their most important symbol of religious life, the temple.

EZEKIEL

Ezekiel was taken to captivity when the Babylonians struck Judah in 597 BC. He began his ministry among the exiles in Babylon, declaring God's judgment would finally crush Judah and the temple. Ezekiel also pronounced God's judgment upon the nations before turning to matters related to the Israelite's repentance and eventual restoration.

DANIEL

Daniel was taken to captivity when the Babylonians struck Judah in 605 BC. Because of his faithfulness, Daniel was exalted to positions of great influence within the new world power, Persia. Through the exploits of Daniel and his friends, the way of faith in the midst of persecution was set forth. And through the wisdom and prophecies of Daniel, God's plan for the ultimate triumph of His kingdom became clear.

To the Southern Kingdom after they returned from Babylon to their land at the decree of King Cyrus of Persia in 538 BC

HAGGAI

After God fulfilled His promise to bring the southern kingdom of Judah back from captivity, the people began rebuilding the temple in Jerusalem. However, it was not long before their priorities got misplaced, and they quit working on the temple for sixteen years. God raised up Haggai to encourage the people to put His work first by completing the temple. Haggai also denounced the people's sin and lifted their sights to the future Messiah's kingdom.

ZECHARIAH

A contemporary of Haggai, Zechariah also encouraged the returned remnant to get back to work on the temple. This book is filled with visions, signs, prophecies, celestial visitors, and the voice of God. Yet, it is also very practical, calling God's people to repentance and hope in the future glory of the Messiah's kingdom.

MALACHI

After the rebuilding of both the temple and the walls in Jerusalem, it did not take long for the people to lapse into their old ways—questioning God's love for them, failing to give Him due honor, intermarrying with foreigners, doubting God's justice, failing to bring their tithes and offerings, and believing that righteous lives were lived in vain. Malachi challenged the people for these sins and ended with a call to obedience and a look forward to when God's messenger would bring repentance.

Three prophets do not fit into the structure reflected above

OBADIAH

Obadiah brought a word of comfort to the southern kingdom of Judah, declaring that their neighbors to the southeast, the Edomites, would be judged by God for their refusal to help Judah in her day of trouble. Though Edom thought they were secure, the Lord declared, "I will bring you down."

JONAH

God called the prophet Jonah to preach repentance to the wicked Ninevites. But Jonah refused and hopped a boat headed in the opposite direction. Through a tumultuous storm and a very large fish, God captured the prophet's attention and, consequently, Jonah made his way to Nineveh. The people received the message and repented. Only then does the reason why Jonah initially refused come to light—he knew His gracious God would forgive the wicked Ninevites, and he did not want that to happen!

NAHUM

Jonah had preached, and the Ninevites had repented. But about one hundred years later, the Assyrians (Nineveh was the capital of Assyria) reverted to their old ways of idolatry, vicious violence, and brute arrogance. In 722 BC, they had defeated the northern kingdom of Israel, and now they were threatening the southern kingdom of Judah. Nahum offered a prophetic voice of encouragement to Judah, announcing that the Assyrians would soon be destroyed. His prophecy eventually came true when the Babylonians defeated the Assyrians in 612 BC.

12. The period between the end of the Old Testament (approximately 400 BC) and the beginning of the New Testament (the ministry of John the Baptist around 30 AD) is often referred to as the <u>Silence Period</u> because there was no prophetic word from God during this time, though God was at work behind the scenes preparing the way for His Son.

Remember, the southern kingdom of Judah returned from Babylonian captivity to rebuild the temple (the book of Ezra) and the walls (the book of Nehemiah) in Jerusalem. The prophets Haggai, Zechariah, and Malachi ministered during this time.

After Malachi prophesied around 425 BC, there were no other voices to be heard for the next four hundred years until the voice of John the Baptist was heard crying out in the wilderness, "Make ready the way of the Lord" (Matthew 3:3).

That four-hundred-year period is often referred to as the Silence Period, simply because there were no inspired prophets ministering during this time. However, it must be noted that God was at work preparing the way for the gospel of His Son.

- God was at work through the influence of the Greeks as the entire region felt the unifying presence of Greek culture and language.

- God was at work though the influence of the Romans as they brought military peace to the region, built extensive roads, and provided a more stable government.

- God was at work among His people, the Jews, as their oppression under the Assyrians, the Babylonians, the Persians, the Greeks, and the Romans had sparked in them a great hope for the coming of Messiah.

13-20: A Broad Overview of The New Testament

13. The New Testament consists of 27 books written by the early followers of Jesus Christ.

The thirty-nine books of the Old Testament were written before the birth of Jesus Christ. Now, Jesus's early followers wrote the twenty-seven books of the New Testament, obviously after His birth, life, death, resurrection, and ascension.

14. The 27 books of the New Testament are divided into 5 Historical Books, 21 Epistles (Letters), and 1 Prophetical Book.

The New Testament is made up of three kinds of books: Historical Books, Epistles (Letters), and a Prophetical Book. The first five books are Historical

Books, the next twenty-one are Epistles, and the final book is a Prophetical Book.

THE BOOKS OF THE NEW TESTAMENT			
HISTORICAL BOOKS	EPISTLES (LETTERS)		PROPHETICAL BOOK
Matthew Mark Luke John Acts	Romans 1 Corinthians 2 Corinthians Galatians Ephesians Philippians Colossians 1 Thessalonians 2 Thessalonians 1 Timothy 2 Timothy Titus Philemon	Hebrews James 1 Peter 2 Peter 1 John 2 John 3 John Jude	Revelation

THE HISTORICAL BOOKS

The five Historical Books are broken down into two sets. The first four are the Gospels that record the birth, life, death, resurrection, and ascension of Jesus Christ. The next book, Acts, records the coming of the Holy Spirit upon the church at Pentecost and the subsequent spread of the gospel through the early church from Jerusalem to Rome.

THE EPISTLES (just a fancy word for letters)

The twenty-one Epistles are also broken down into two sets. The first thirteen are referred to as the Pauline Epistles because the Apostle Paul wrote them. The next eight are referred to as Non-Pauline Epistles, because various authors wrote them.

THE PROPHETICAL BOOK

The final book of the New Testament—and of the Bible for that matter—is the Prophetical Book of Revelation, which teaches what will take place in the future.

15. The Gospels present the life and ministry of Jesus Christ from the unique perspectives of four different <u>authors</u> writing to four different <u>audiences</u> with four different <u>purposes</u> in mind, and together they illuminate the majesty of our Savior.

MATTHEW

Matthew wrote his Gospel primarily to a Jewish audience. He traced the genealogy of Jesus Christ back to Abraham and David and demonstrated through multiple Old Testament quotes how Jesus fulfilled Old Testament promises. Matthew sought to persuade his audience that Jesus was the Messiah and to describe the nature of His kingdom in light of the vast Jewish rejection of Christ.

MARK

Mark wrote his Gospel primarily to a Roman audience. This Gospel focuses more on the actions of Jesus than on His teaching, because Mark desired to present Jesus as the servant who came to suffer and give His life for others. Mark also sought to teach that those who follow Jesus must be willing to suffer the same fate.

LUKE

Luke wrote his Gospel primarily to a Greek audience. Wrought through painstaking research, this Gospel records the story of Jesus in great detail and chronological accuracy. Luke presented Jesus as the Savior for all, demonstrating Jesus's desire to seek and save those from all social classes. He healed the sick and preached the gospel to the poor and needy. He reached out to sinful women, to despised tax collectors, and to the down and out.

JOHN

John wrote his Gospel primarily to the world. This Gospel is the most theological of the four, demonstrating that Jesus is in fact the Son of God. Seven "I am" statements reveal His Person: He is the "bread of life"; "the light of the world"; "the door"; "the good shepherd"; "the resurrection and the life"; "the way, the truth, and the life"; and "the true vine." Seven signs reveal His power and validate His claims: He changed water into wine, healed the official's son, healed the invalid at Bethesda, fed the five thousand, walked on water, healed the man born blind, and raised Lazarus from the dead. John declared his purpose in writing, "Therefore many other signs Jesus also performed in the presence of the disciples, which are not written in this book; but these have been written so that you may believe that Jesus is the Christ, the Son of God; and that believing you may have life in His name." (John 20:30–31)

From a big-picture perspective, each of the four Gospels covers the life, teaching, death, and resurrection of Jesus. But, each one does so from a distinct perspective, and together they paint a grand portrait of the Savior.

16. The book of Acts records the spread of the church from its birth (1:1–2:43) and expansion in <u>Jerusalem</u> (3:1–6:7) to its extension into <u>Judea and Samaria</u> (6:8–9:31), <u>Antioch</u> (9:32–12:24), <u>Asia Minor</u> (12:25–16:5), the <u>Aegean Sea</u> region (16:6–19:20), and <u>Rome</u> (19:21–28:31). Each movement is summarized with a progress report from Luke.

Acts is the only book that picks up where the Gospels left off, answering, "What happened after Jesus ascended into heaven?" The answer we find is that after Jesus ascended into heaven, He sent the Holy Spirit into the lives of His followers, and through them, the church spread from Jerusalem all the way to Rome.

Luke organized this story of the birth, expansion, and spread of the church with progress reports found throughout the book. First, we read of the birth of the church in Acts 1:1–2:47, and then Luke reported in 2:47b, "And the Lord was adding to their number day by day those who were being saved." In Acts 3:1–6:7, we see the gospel's influence expand within Jerusalem as the early followers of Jesus "filled the city with their teaching." Luke then summarized in 6:7, "The word of God kept on spreading; and the number of the disciples continued to increase greatly in Jerusalem, and a great many of the priests were becoming obedient to the faith."

Next, the church spread into the surrounding regions of Judea and Samaria in 6:8–9:31, and then Luke reported in 9:31, "So the church throughout all Judea and Galilee and Samaria enjoyed peace, being built up; and going on in the fear of the Lord and in the comfort of the Holy Spirit, it continued to increase." The church then spread north to Antioch in 9:32–12:24 before Luke summarized, "But the word of the Lord continued to grow and to be multiplied."

Next, the missionary journeys of Paul started, and the church spread into Asia Minor in 12:25–16:5. Luke wrote in 16:5, "So the churches were being strengthened in the faith, and were increasing in number daily." The church then spread to the regions surrounding the Aegean Sea in 16:6–19:20. Luke recorded the progress in 19:20, "So the word of the Lord was growing mightily and prevailing." Finally, the church spread to Rome in 19:21–28:31.

Luke summarized this progress and closed the book, "And he stayed two full years in his own rented quarters and was welcoming all who came to him, preaching the kingdom of God and teaching concerning the Lord Jesus Christ with all openness, unhindered."

In Acts, Jesus gave His final instructions, ascended into heaven, gave the Holy Spirit to His followers, and through them spread His gospel-formed church from Jerusalem all the way to Rome.

ACTS
Written by Luke, the book of Acts records the spread of the gospel throughout the Mediterranean world. In obedience to Jesus's instructions, after being filled with the Holy Spirit, the early believers proclaimed the gospel to the city of Jerusalem, the surrounding regions of Judea and Samaria, and the remotest parts of the earth through the missionary journeys of the Apostle Paul. The story is one of strong faith, earnest prayer, and great courage.

17. The Pauline letters are best understood in their historical context: After his First Missionary Journey, Paul wrote <u>Galatians</u>; during his Second Journey, he wrote <u>1 Thessalonians</u> and <u>2 Thessalonians</u>; during his Third Journey, he wrote <u>1 Corinthians</u>, <u>2 Corinthians</u>, and <u>Romans</u>. During his first imprisonment in Rome, he wrote <u>Ephesians</u>, <u>Colossians</u>, <u>Philemon</u>, and <u>Philippians</u>; after his release from prison, he wrote <u>1 Timothy</u> and <u>Titus</u>; finally, during his second imprisonment in Rome, not long before his death, he wrote <u>2 Timothy</u>.

Paul's letters, Romans through Philemon, are generally arranged from longest to shortest. But, it is often helpful to understand how they fit historically into his life and ministry. Acts 13-28 records the three missionary journeys of the Apostle Paul and his "fourth" journey as a prisoner to Rome. It was during those missionary journeys, his first imprisonment in Rome, and further ministry and imprisonment that Paul's letters were written. And God's providence helps us remember these as Paul wrote one book after his first journey, two books during his second, three books during his third, and four books during his "fourth." He then wrote three other books after his "fourth" journey as a prisoner to Rome.

THE EPISTLES OF THE APOSTLE PAUL			
Circumstance	Book(s) Written	Approximate Date (AD)	Place of Writing
1st Missionary Journey	Galatians	48-49 After 1st Journey	Antioch of Syria
2nd Missionary Journey	1 Thessalonians 2 Thessalonians	51 51-52 During 2nd Journey	Corinth Corinth
3rd Missionary Journey	1 Corinthians 2 Corinthians Romans	56 56 56-57 During 3rd Journey	Ephesus Macedonia Corinth
"4th" Missionary Journey 1st Imprisonment	Ephesians Colossians Philemon Philippians	60 61 61 62 During Imprisonment	Rome Rome Rome Rome
After Release from Prison	1 Timothy Titus	62 66 After Release	Macedonia? Macedonia?
During Last Imprisonment	2 Timothy	67 During Imprisonment	Rome

After Paul's First Missionary Journey, he returned to Antioch and wrote Galatians.

GALATIANS

After preaching Christ and planting churches in the southern region of Galatia, Paul received word that false teachers had moved in and were destroying his work. They were questioning Paul's authority as an apostle and teaching a false gospel. Paul wrote Galatians to defend his apostleship and his gospel of God's grace, as well as to encourage his readers to live the Christian life in the power of the Holy Spirit.

During his Second Missionary Journey, Paul wrote both 1 and 2 Thessalonians from Corinth.

1 THESSALONIANS
After ministering in Thessalonica and moving on to Athens, Paul sent Timothy to Thessalonica to check in with the believers, and then Paul moved on to Corinth. Upon Timothy's return and report, Paul wrote 1 Thessalonians to commend the faith, love, and hope of the believers, defend his ministry against false accusations, and call his readers to greater excellence in Christian living.

2 THESSALONIANS
While still in Corinth, some time after writing 1 Thessalonians, Paul received another report from the church. This time, they had questions concerning the day of the Lord and the antichrist. Paul wrote 2 Thessalonians to answer their questions and call them to hope in the future triumph of Jesus despite their difficult circumstances.

During Paul's Third Missionary Journey, he wrote 1 Corinthians from Ephesus. He later moved on to Macedonia and wrote 2 Corinthians. He eventually made it to Corinth where he wrote Romans.

1 CORINTHIANS
It appears that 1 Corinthians was preceded by a "previous letter" of which we have no record (1 Corinthians 5:9-11). Paul wrote 1 Corinthians to correct these erring believers in matters related to factions within the church, unchallenged immorality in their midst (the message of his "previous letter" in 5:9-11), unjustified lawsuits among believers, and sexual immorality. He then responded to a number of questions the church had related to marriage and divorce, meat sacrificed to idols, the Lord's Supper, spiritual gifts, and the resurrection of Jesus.

2 CORINTHIANS
It appears that 2 Corinthians was preceded by a "painful visit" unrecorded in Acts (2 Corinthians 2:1) and a "severe letter" of which we also have no record (2 Corinthians 2:4). Having left Ephesus to rendezvous with Titus and hear how the

Corinthians had responded to his "severe letter," Paul received word in Macedonia that they had responded well. He then wrote 2 Corinthians to express his joy at their repentance, encourage them to give financially to the burdened believers in Jerusalem, and still defend himself against some within Corinth who challenged his apostolic authority.

ROMANS

Paul was anxious to preach Christ in Rome and possibly establish this city as a headquarters for future missionary activity. From Corinth, just before going to Jerusalem with the monetary gift for the suffering saints, Paul wrote Romans in preparation for his coming. In his most systematic letter, Paul set forth his theology as he established the condemnation of all because of sin, the justification of believers through the gospel, the sanctification of believers by means of union with Christ and the indwelling Holy Spirit, the vindication of God related to Israel's present rejection and future repentance, and the application of the gospel to everyday life.

Paul's "fourth missionary journey" took him to Rome as a prisoner. While spending time in house arrest for about two years, Paul wrote four letters, most likely in this order—Ephesians, Colossians, Philemon, and Philippians.

EPHESIANS

In the book of Ephesians, Paul spent the first three chapters focused on the believers' great calling before spending the last three focused on their conduct. In the first portion of the letter, Paul set forth God's work of salvation that was accomplished for believers' eternal good and the demonstration of God's glorious grace. In the latter portion of the letter, Paul called his readers to a faithful Christian "walk"—a "walk" in unity, holiness, love, light, and wisdom. Finally, he called them to "stand firm."

COLOSSIANS

In the book of Colossians, Paul again spent the first half focused on Christian doctrine before spending the second half on Christian duty. After commending the believers for their faith and love, Paul exalted the supremacy of Jesus Christ in both His person and His work. He also called believers to practice true spirituality, which is focused on Jesus and not legalistic rules. He spent the last two chapters on practical Christian living.

PHILEMON

Onesimus was a runaway slave that Paul converted to Christianity while in Rome. Now, in faithfulness to Christ, Onesimus felt compelled to return to his master, Philemon. Paul penned this letter urging Philemon to accept Onesimus, whom Paul had grown to love as a useful servant in the gospel, no longer as a slave, but as a beloved brother. Paul pledged that he would repay anything that Onesimus owed to Philemon.

PHILIPPIANS

Still in prison, Paul was consumed with the joy of the Lord. He wrote Philippians to commend and thank the church for their financial support of his ministry. He also urged these believers to pursue Christian harmony as relationships within the church were suffering. They were to exercise the kind of humility toward others as exemplified by Jesus Christ who left heaven's glory, became a man, and died for others. Paul also provided a great example of contentment as he learned the secret, "I can do all things through Him who strengthens me."

The book of Acts ends in chapter 28 with Paul in Rome under house arrest. The remaining history of his life must be pieced together from things gleaned from his final letters. Most scholars believe Paul was released from house arrest in Rome after which he carried on further missionary work. During this time of ministry, he wrote 1 Timothy and Titus.

1 TIMOTHY

After leaving Timothy as leader of the church in Ephesus, Paul wrote to instruct his young protégé who faced the daunting task of leading the church. Paul urged Timothy to meet head on issues related to false teachers, disorder in worship, qualified leadership, pastoral responsibility, widows in the church, materialism, and more.

TITUS

Like Timothy in Ephesus, Paul left Titus on the island of Crete to lead the cause of Christ. Paul wrote to instruct Titus concerning the appointment of qualified elders in each local church as well as the need to instruct God's people to live influential lives inspired by God's grace and humbled by God's kindness, love, and mercy.

Finally, Paul was arrested again and taken to a much harsher imprisonment, in Rome. During this imprisonment, Paul wrote his final letter, 2 Timothy. Soon after writing, Paul was beheaded.

2 TIMOTHY
Paul was taken back into prison for the last time. He was cold, somewhat lonely, and the stench of death hung in the air. Paul wrote Timothy as a father to a son, a mentor to a protégé, urging him to courageously fulfill his ministry even in the face of hardship, knowing Christ will reward His faithful servants. In this small but motivating book, Paul charged Timothy to kindle afresh the gift within him, suffer hardship for the gospel, continue in the truth, proclaim the word, fight the good fight, finish the course, and keep the faith.

18. The Non-Pauline Letters were written by <u>various</u> authors, some to more <u>general</u> audiences (these letters are often called the General Epistles) and together, they supplement Paul's teaching by offering additional perspectives on the <u>richness</u> of Christian truth and life.[9]

HEBREWS
An unknown author wrote this letter to a mainly Jewish audience to encourage them to remain faithful to Jesus Christ in the face of persecution. Many were tempted to abandon their Christian commitment and go back to their old ways under Judaism. In an effort to encourage faithfulness to the Lord, the author established the supremacy of Jesus Christ and warned against rejecting Him.

JAMES
James, the Lord's brother, wrote to call his readers to put their faith into practice. Unlike Paul's letters which often focus on doctrine before turning to practice, James jumped right into practical matters as he addressed topics such as trials, temptation, faith and works, the tongue, worldliness, planning, riches, and prayer.

1 PETER
Peter's readers were suffering both the mysterious trials of life and the sneers and ostracism of persecution. He wrote to remind his readers of their glorious salvation, the purpose of their trials, and their calling to holiness and love. And

he encouraged them to live with excellence as citizens, employees, spouses, and persecuted Christians so that their behavior would be distinct and influential in the culture.

2 PETER

In this letter, Peter called his readers away from a stagnant faith to one of continual growth that proves one useful in the cause of Christ. He warned of false prophets, taught of the false teachers' sure destruction, and challenged his readers to grow in the knowledge of Jesus Christ so they might be on guard against erroneous teaching.

1 JOHN

John wanted to reassure his readers that they indeed possessed eternal life. To do so, John weaved through this letter three tests by which this could be determined—love for other believers, obedience to God, and belief in Jesus Christ. In matter-of-fact, black-and-white fashion, John asserted that salvation is evidenced by love for others in the family of God, obedience to the will of God (not perfection, but direction), and proper belief in Jesus. If a person possesses these things, then that person shows evidence of belonging to God. If a person does not possess these things, then that person shows evidence of not belonging to God.

2 JOHN

John addressed this letter to a local church (the chosen lady) and its members (her children), encouraging them to continue strong in the truth about Jesus Christ. John warned of false teachers who sought to infiltrate the church and called the believers to stand strong against their error.

3 JOHN

In this letter, John commended the recipient, Gaius, for his commitment to the truth and his love for the church. He encouraged Gaius to continue supporting faithful missionaries, and then addressed issues related to two men—Diotrephes, the unfaithful and Demetrius, the faithful.

JUDE

Jude wrote to charge his readers to "contend" for the faith in the face of false teaching. After demonstrating the sure destruction of false teachers, Jude encouraged the believers to a life of truth, prayer, hope, and ministry.

19. Revelation is the final book of the Bible and records the vision of Jesus John saw (1:12–16), Jesus's letters to the seven churches of John's day (Ch. 2–3), and the things that will take place in the future (Ch. 4–22), most clearly the Second Coming of Jesus Christ and the life everlasting for both the saved and the unsaved.

Revelation 1:19 seems to outline the contents of this book: "Therefore, write the things which you have seen, and the things which are, and the things which will take place after these things."

- "The things which you have seen" refers to the specific vision of the resurrected and exalted Christ which John records in Revelation 1:12–16.

- "The things which are" refers to the letters that Jesus dictated to seven churches of John's day—the churches in Ephesus, Smyrna, Pergamum, Thyatira, Sardis, Philadelphia, and Laodicea. John recorded these words from Jesus in Revelation 2:1–3:22.

- "The things which will take place after these things" refers to the remainder of the book that sets forth the coming rise of antichrist, the tribulation, the second coming of Jesus, His kingdom, the great white throne judgment, and the eternal state. John recorded these things in Revelation 4:1–22:21.

Having said that, many good, Bible-believing theologians differ on how best to interpret the book of Revelation. Some would even disagree with my description of the book above. But all good, Bible-believing Christians agree on two main points when it comes to the future—Jesus Christ will return to this earth one day, and those who know Him will spend eternity with Him while those who refuse His salvation will spend eternity separated from Him.

REVELATION
To inspire both holiness and hope in his readers, the Apostle John penned this book to believers located in seven cities in Asia Minor. At the instruction of the Lord, John recorded "the things which he had seen" (the vision of the exalted Lord Jesus), "the things which are" (Jesus's letters of commendation and confrontation to the seven churches), and "the things which must take place after these things" (the tribulation, rise of antichrist, second coming of

Jesus, establishment of the kingdom, final rebellion of Satan, great white throne judgment, and eternal state).

20. Get a grip on the Bible by <u>hearing</u>, <u>reading</u>, <u>studying</u>, <u>memorizing</u>, <u>meditating on</u>, and <u>applying</u> the Bible for a lifetime.

There are six disciplines one must cultivate to become a person strong in the Scriptures.

HEAR THE WORD

Every Christian needs to cultivate the discipline of hearing the word of God, whether it is being read or being taught. There are great resources available like the Bible on CD and of course online, which allow a person to hear the word of God over and over. Also, all Christians need to avail themselves of good Bible teaching—through audio resources, but most importantly in their own local churches.

READ THE WORD

It is not enough for a Christian simply to hear the word of God read or taught. Each Christian must also cultivate the personal discipline of Reading the Word. Reading the Word refers to working through books of the Bible at a decent pace. It is sitting down and reading Genesis over the course of a week or two. It is setting aside 30 minutes to read through Paul's letter to the Ephesians. It is simply Reading the Bible.

STUDY THE WORD

It is not enough to hear and read the word of God. The Christian must also study God's word. If reading is working through books of the Bible at a decent pace, then Studying the Word is working through passages of the Bible slowly but surely. It involves a pen and paper in hand, making note of key words, pondering relationships between paragraphs, doing word studies, etc. Reading the Word is like flying over a city to get the "lay of the land." Studying the Word is like getting out of the plane and walking the streets to become much more familiar with the surroundings.

MEMORIZE THE WORD

It is not enough to hear, read, and study the word of God. The Christian must also cultivate the discipline of Memorizing the Word. The psalmist said, "Your Word I have treasured in my heart that I may not sin against You" (Psalm 119:11). This involves taking favorite verses, pertinent passages, and even whole books of the Bible, and working diligently to store them up in your mind. In spiritual warfare with Satan, Jesus quoted Scripture that He had memorized (Matthew 4:1-11).

MEDITATE ON THE WORD

It is not enough to hear, read, study, and memorize the word of God. The Christian must also meditate on God's word. Meditating on the Word is totally distinct from new-age-type meditation that encourages the emptying of the mind. Biblical meditation rather encourages believers to fill their minds with God's truth, running the thoughts of God's word through their minds over and over. The psalmist said of the godly person, "But his delight is in the law of the Lord, and in His law he meditates day and night" (Psalm 1:2).

APPLY THE WORD

Finally, it's not even enough to hear, read, study, memorize, and meditate on the word of God. The Christian must move on to applying the word of God. Is there a sin to avoid? Is there a promise to claim? Is there an example to follow? Is there a command to obey? Is there a prayer to express? What does this passage teach about God, ourselves, what God has done, and how we should respond?

Notes

1. "The Mind of God," Bible.org, accessed October 17, 2017, https://bible.org/illustration/mind-god.

2. Max Anders, *30 Days to Understanding the Bible* (Nashville, Tennessee: Thomas Nelson Inc., 2011), 30-31.

3. J. Hampton Keathley, III. "The Non-Pauline Epistles" posted on August 4, 2004, http://bible.org/article/non-pauline-epistles. I like the way Keathley says, "They supplement the thirteen Pauline Epistles by offering different perspectives on the richness of Christian truth."

4. Charles Cladwell Ryrie, *Basic Theology: A Popular Systematic Guide to Understanding Biblical Truth* (Chicago, Illinois: Moody Publishers, 1999), 71.

5. Norman L. Geisler, ed., *Inerrancy* (Grand Rapids, Michigan: Zondervan Publishing House, 1980), 294.

6. Wayne A. Grudem, *Systematic Theology: An Introduction to Biblical Doctrine* (Leicester, England: Inter-Varsity Press, 1994), 73.

7. Josh McDowell, *The New Evidence That Demands a Verdict* (Nashville, Tennessee: Thomas Nelson, 1999), 3-7.

8. Anders, *30 Days to Understanding the Bible*, 30-31.

9. J. Hampton Keathley, III, "The Non-Pauline Epistles." I like the way Keathley says, "They supplement the thirteen Pauline Epistles by offering different perspectives on the richness of Christian truth."

CLARIFYING
THE BIBLE

GET THE DIGITAL VIDEO DOWNLOAD FOR
FREE WITH COUPON BELOW.

JUST FOLLOW THESE EASY STEPS:

1. GO TO **CLARIFYINGTHEBIBLE.COM**

2. CLICK ON THE **STORE** TAB

3. ADD ALL THE SESSIONS TO YOUR CART

4. ENTER **CLARIFYING01** AS THE COUPON CODE AND CLICK
APPLY COUPON

5. CHECK OUT

CPSIA information can be obtained
at www.ICGtesting.com
Printed in the USA
JSHW021114080320
4612JS00005B/14